BEYOND
EXPANDING OUR IDEAS
OF WHAT IS POSSIBLE

Serena Rosemary Scholz

Copyright © 2012
by Serena Rosemary Scholz

ISBN 978-1-105-78618-1

All Rights Reserved.

*To all the wonderful people
who know and support me,
and to all the people
I hope to meet in the future.*

Impossible is just a big word
thrown around by
small men
who find it easier
to live in the world they have been given
than to explore the power they have
to change it.

Impossible is not a fact.
It's an opinion.

Impossible is not a declaration.
It's a dare.

Impossible is potential.

Impossible is temporary,

Impossible is nothing.

-The Difference Maker
J. Maxwell

Contents

Introduction

Knowledge

Endurance

Compassion

Embers

Sight

Cells

Martial Arts

Song

Necessities

Navigation

Heart

INTRODUCTION

I'm trying something new here with this book. Please bear with me for a moment, but this isn't going to be like anything you might have read before.

I think the difference is that I'm not looking for answers. So many books (and people) are just looking for the simple answer. If the answer was simple, wouldn't we have found it by now?

What if I said I don't always believe in perfect answers?

This book is not just going to be a barrage of information assaulting your brain. No formulas, no endings, probably not even any perfect conclusions. These stories are short, with lots of room for interested thinkers to work with them. All I'm doing is trying to get the underlying message across to you, and to communicate the reason I decided to do this in the first place. It's not just because I think these things are cool (which they are), but because I wanted to let you know that there are still things in the world that people just don't understand. No one understands them. They're like magic.

You've probably gotten to a point in your life now when you say, "Oh, I don't believe in magic anymore." You may even put this book back on the shelf because it mentions such a ridiculous thing. But let me tell you, every single thing in this book is wholly and entirely real. That is not open for debate – these are proven, tested, witnessed things.

Whether or not you want to call them magic is your own choice, of course.

We live in a world that is becoming more and more scientific and technology-obsessed. This isn't a judgment on my part, just a fact. We're not only breaking atoms but breaking subatomic particles, because we want to know how everything works, how everything functions. We want the whole universe to work according our models and equations.

So when we come across something that is blatantly "not possible," but is still *happening*, we have two options. We either fix something in our equations to try to accommodate it, or we just ignore it.

Unfortunately, it's more common for these things just to be ignored. And this is exactly the reason why I wrote this book. I want you to know there are things that people can't explain, no matter how hard we try.

Why do I want you to know that? Because if you don't believe in things that can't be explained, your whole world is made smaller by the ideas of what is real, and what is "possible." And if you don't have any limits on what is supposedly "possible," then everything is! There are no limits anymore, no bounds on possibility.

    Cool, right?

> – Serena Rosemary Scholz
> 2012

I would rather have a mind
<u>o p e n e d</u>
by
<u>w o n d e r</u>

than one
[closed   ]
by
belief.

-George Spence

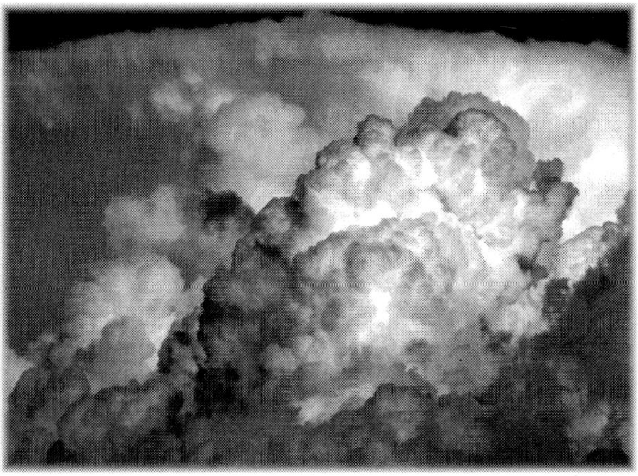

On
KNOWLEDGE

The Dogon tribe is one of the most ancient groups of people in Africa. They have a long, rich history, with astrological lore that goes back as far as 3200 BCE. Living in small communities in the center of Mali, they have managed to keep their traditional ways alive despite the quick modernization of the world around them.

In the late 1930s, two French anthropologists went to learn about the Dogon culture. Their names were Marcel Griaule and Germain Dieterlen.

Marcel and Germain talked to a Dogon priest about the ancient stories, recording them for further study and research. Much of the tribe's mythology is based on the star Sirius, which is also called the Dog Star. According to the Dogon traditions, the star Sirius has a twin star, which is invisible to the eye. The Dogon said that the companion star is very dense and heavy, and that it has an elliptical orbit around Sirius, and makes a complete orbit every fifty years. They also knew the star rotates on its axis. To this day, the

Dogon hold a huge celebration every fifty years to mark the end of the invisible star's orbit.

This may not seem to be very important. It might not be – if it wasn't completely true. The companion star (Sirius B, as it was later named) wasn't 'discovered' by Western astronomers until the 1980s, when the newest high powered telescope saw a tiny wobble in the path of Sirius, caused by the graviational pull of its invisible companion star. How could a tribe with no such technology have known this? Their dusty villages in Mali, made up of small huts with dirt floors, don't exactly boast of their technological prowess. So how could they have known this obscure fact about the universe?

Some skpetics believe that the Westerners must have discussed astrology with the Dogon priests before Marcel and Germaine visited them. This might be, because in 1844 an astronomer in Europe had an idea that Sirius might have a twin. His theory later vanish, not resurfacing until the star was found. But this doesn't account for the fact that a 400-year-old Dogon artifact shows the formation of the Sirius stars. Or the fact that the Dogon have been holding celebrations based on the orbits Sirius A and B since the 11th century. It also doesn't explain how they knew about the super density of the second star. Sirius B is called a white dwarf star, and is so heavy that one teaspoon of it on

Earth would weigh five tons or 10,000 pounds.

When the Dogon were later asked how they knew such an astounding thing, their answer was once again far from ordinary. According to their history, the tribe were given the information by a race called the Nommos, who visited Earth thousands of years ago. The Nommos told them about the cycles of Sirius and Sirius B, and also about a third star in the system. This third star was supposedly the home planet of the Nommos. The Nommos were described as fish men and women, much like the mer-people of many ancient stories.

Most scientists think that there is not a third star. However, in 1995, two astronomers wrote a journal entitled, "Is Sirius a Triple Star?" The writers argued that based on the movements of the system, they suspect that there *is* a very small third object. The question may be settled forever with the invention of a higher-powered telescope. But until then, we may never know the secrets of Dogon astronomy.

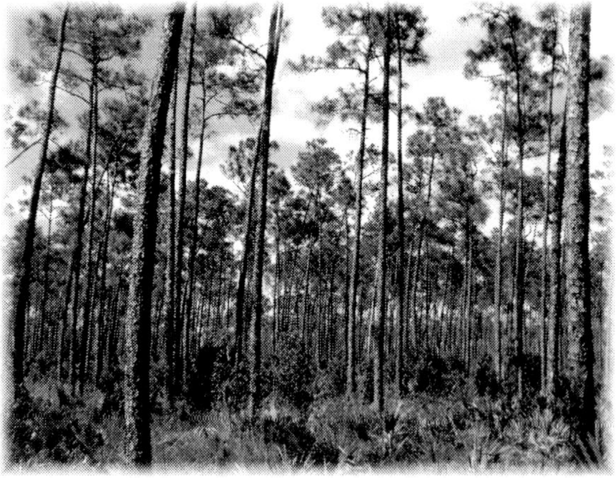

The men who learn
endurance
are those who call the
whole world
brother.

-Charles Dickens

On
ENDURANCE

Not many people can boast that they have run a full marathon, a race over 26 miles long. Wim Hof is one of these people. However, his marathon was more extraordinary than most.

The marathon was run above the Arctic Circle, where temperatures get to -4°F. And Wim Hof ran the entire 26 miles, through snow and on top of tundra, in bare feet and shorts.

Hof, who was born in the Netherlands, has somehow developed a strange immunity to the cold. He sucessfully climbed Africa's Mt. Kilimanjaro in his swim trunks, and made it almost all the way up Nepal's Mt. Everest in shorts and a tshirt before he injured his foot and had to descend. As a stunt, he buried himself in pounds of ice up to his neck for ninety minutes – setting a world record for the longest ice bath. This ability to withstand cold is not only strange, it is way beyond the limits of what we think an ordinary person can bear. A regular person placed in the bath of ice that Hof sat in for an hour and a half would be dead from hypothermia in minutes.

The "Iceman" was not born with his

ability. As he tells his story, it first started when he was about twenty three. He was walking in a park with a date in the middle of December, and they stopped at a half frozen pond. "I saw the ice and I thought, what would happen if I go in there," he said. "I was really attracted to it. I went in, got rid of my clothes. Tremendous good feeling when I came out and since then, I repeated it every day."

Hof was studied at the University of Minnesota hypothermia lab later in his life. When they asked him what it felt like to sit in the ice bath, or be in such extreme temperatures, he said that it felt normal to him. He said that, in his mind, he is able to turn a "mental thermostat" that regulates the rest of his body's heat. When he is in a cold place, he simply "turns the thermostat up."

While this explanation may sound completely ridiculous to the scientists, Hof is not the first person to do such things. In Tibet, a sect of monks have been practicing the art of *tuomo*, which means inner fire, since the 8th century. *Tuomo* is a form of yoga in which the mind controls the heat of the body, and therefore is able to tell the body to produce much more heat than it usually can. The monks meditate in only shorts out in the snowy Tibetan mountains, and just like Wim Hof, they don't seem to feel the cold at all. True testaments to the power of *tuomo* are the initiation rites of the Tibetan monastery: the man or woman who wishes to enter the order is placed, naked, out on the snow and ice in late evening. He is then covered with six heavy wool blankets, each soaked through with cold water. The only instructions given are to have the blankets dry by morning. Temperatures in Tibet get down to -50°F at night, a temperature that no human being can supposedly bear, especially not unclothed and under six soaking wet wool blankets.

Some initiates die. However, most have enough training in *tuomo* that they are able to generate sufficient body heat to not only live, but dry the blankets completely by the time they are met by their new community in the morning. The modern science of physiology does little to help us understand these remarkable abilites.

When we know ourselves to be
connected to all others,
acting
c o m p a s s i o n a t e l y
is simply the
<u>natural thing</u>
to do.

- Rachel Naomi Remen

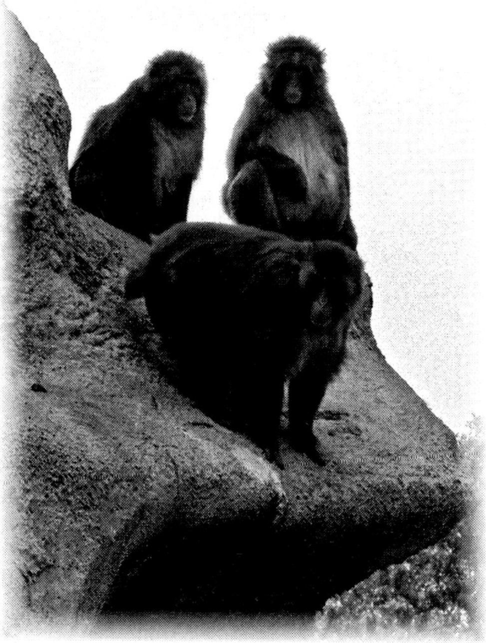

On
COMPASSION

Returning to her home after a day at work, a woman was kidnapped and shoved into a pickup truck by a man wearing a mask. She was gagged and blindfolded. The man told her that he was going to kill her.

The truck ride took a long time. As the woman waited in the back, she was terrified. And so she began to go through the phases of fear. The first stage is denial. She thought that maybe she was having a bad dream. She pinched herself, tried to tell herself that it was just an elaborate prank.

But soon she couldn't pretend anymore. She moved onto the next stage of fear, which is anger. "This is so unfair!" she thought. She kicked and screamed, trying to loosen the ropes that held her down.

After a while, she had to give the anger up too. The next stage was bargaining. She struggled to get the man to remove the gag, and when he did she began trying to keep her life by promising him things – money, help, freedom. She promised that she wouldn't even tell the police if he let her go.

The man didn't listen, and stuffed the cloth back into her mouth. She sat in the forced darkness, the blindfold tightly bound over her eyes, and descended into the fourth stage, depression. She sat silent, like a stone, mind numb.

As she sat quietly, she slid without knowing into the fifth stage: acceptance.

And from acceptance, she went into compassion. She wondered sadly what had hurt this man so badly that he would take another human's life.

Suddenly, the truck stopped. The man ripped the blindfold off, and she saw that they were in an empty marsh. The grasses were a dead light brown and blowing in the cold wind. The trees were bare. It was late autumn and the leaves were all gone in preparation for the snow to come.

He took the gag out of her mouth. He told her to kneel down.

She sat on the cold grass. He looked down at her, a pistol gleaming in his hand. She looked up into his eyes, hair blown by the wind across her eyes. He raised the gun.

"Wait," she said. She was trying to be calm still, to hold onto her acceptance. But she couldn't stop her voice from shaking.

"Before you kill me," she said, "I want you to know that I'm really… sorry. I'm sorry that something in your life is so terrible you feel like you need to kill someone. I'm sorry you feel desperate enough to do this. I just want you… to know… that I feel for you." She looked up at his eyes. Shock registered.

Then all of a sudden, the man sat down on the ground and began to weep.

He drove her back to the nearest subway station, and even gave her money to pay the fare. She arrived back at her home later that evening, and never heard from him again.

We should be reminded that compassion is a gift for which we all have a huge capacity.

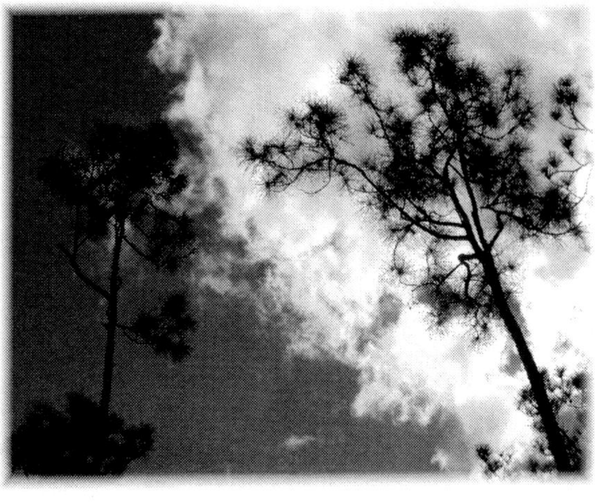

What we can or cannot do,
what we consider possible or impossible,
is rarely a function of our true capability.
It is more likely
**a function of our beliefs
about who we are.**

- Tony Robbins

On
__E__MBERS

In the center of a small village in Sri Lanka, a huge pit lies empty. The hole is ten feet deep and three times as long, and is used for a community celebration.

Every year, the people of the village build a huge fire that fills the pit entirely. They leave it to burn, and the fire roars for days until it is reduced to just the embers.

These coals are white hot. A piece of paper thrown into the pit bursts into flames four inches before it even hits them. Aluminum, which melts at 1220°F, is reduced to molten liquid as soon as it touches the bed of embers. There has been speculation that the coals may be over 2000°F.

The fire and coals are to honor the local deities, or gods. The villagers gathers around the coals to laugh, sing, and dance, rejoicing in the harvest and prosperity of their village. After the celebration, every woman, man, and child in the village is led in a sacred ritual. They clear their minds of any thoughts, and fill their bodies with gratefulness to the gods and to the world. When they are ready, every single person in the village, men, women and children, form a loose line and jump into the pit, walking barefooted into the thousand-degree bed of coals.

When they reach the other side, their feet have not been burned at all.

Success isn't about
what you *accomplish* in your life
it's about what you
i n s p i re
others
to do.

-Unknown

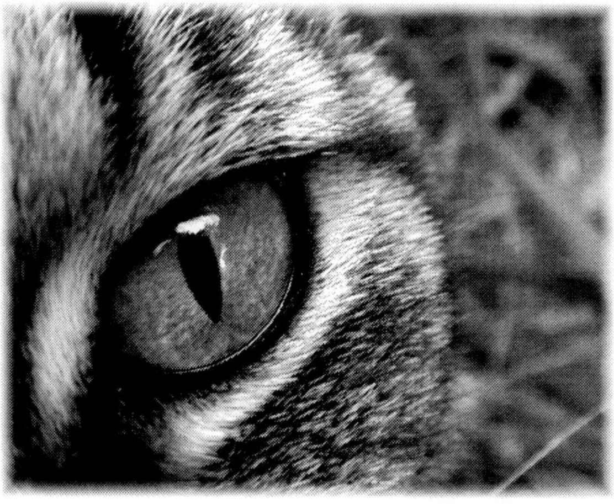

On
SIGHT

In the late 1950's, strange ads started to appear in the newspapers. A man named Kuda Bux placed numerous calls for free demonstrations of psychic power and x-ray vision. People were skeptical. Not many went. But the few who did were changed forever.

These small demonstrations were held by Mr. Bux and his wife in a rented lecture hall. They were completely free of charge, with no registration of any kind required. Mr. Bux was self sufficient, and he said the only reason he was holding these gatherings was to inform people that they had a far greater capacity as human beings than they knew.

* * *

Mr. Bux stands up in front of the people assembled. There are usually no more than two dozen seated in folding chairs. He takes out a deck of cards, and begins:

"I want to show you some card tricks," he says, "because I want you to understand the difference between tricks and reality." He performs a simple trick, then shows how he hid the disappearing card up his sleeve. "This is a trick," he tells the audience.

Setting down the cards, he continues, "and this next bit is reality."

He asks for two volunteers from the audience and brings out a large cardboard box. From the box, he takes two large pieces of floury bread dough. He kneads them for a moment before handing them to the volunteers. "Put these over my eyes," he instructs them.

The squishy dough molds into his eye sockets easily, covering up his eyes entirely. Next, he takes two huge sheets of cotton, and instructs the volunteers to place them over the dough. The cotton is then taped on with medical tape. As if that was not enough, he next has them take out a huge black cloth. As per his instructions, they check it thoroughly, making certain that Mr. Bux can not see through any part of it. This is tied around his head very tightly, with a strong knot.

At this point, it looks like Mr. Bux's head is completely mummified. But to show even the extreme skeptics in the audience, the last step is a huge black velvet bag. The volunteers examine it, deducing that it is not a trick bag either. They put it over his head, and he tells them to draw the drawstring tight around his chin and neck.

Satisfied that they have done a good job in completely incapacitating Mr. Bux's eyes, the volunteers return to the audience.

Mrs. Bux enters, carrying a large box of colorful balloons. One by one she picks up a different color balloon, and one by one he tells her and the audience what color it is. Next, he has people from the audience pick the balloons. He doesn't miss one.

He pulls a needle and thread out of his pocket, and proceeds to thread it in one try.

"Does anyone here have a book?" He asks. A girl in the audience raised her hand. "Bring it down here please," he says. When she gets to the front of the group, he asks her to open it to any page. She complies. To the astonishment of everyone there, he begins to read.

He has seven or eight people in the audience each pick pages of the book for him to read, and he complies without fault. The people are flabbergasted.

For the last part of his demonstration, he has anyone who has not yet been a volunteer come to the front. He asks each person to write a sentence on the blackboard. The first person writes, "Can you read this?" He laughs, says yes, and then, with a piece of chalk, goes over every single letter, exactly as it is written on the board. When he reaches the "i" in this, he notes, "You forgot to dot the i," and adds a small dot.

Each volunteer then writes a sentence, and each sentence he carefully traces over with his own piece of chalk. Halfway through, he asks if anyone knows another language, and for them please to write something on the board. A Middle Eastern woman writes a long sentence in Arabic, and he traces over the letters and symbols, one by one.

The audience returns to their seats, and Bux pulls a pair of glasses out of his suit pocket. His head is still completely mummified. "With my physical eyes," he said, "I must use glasses to read and write. But otherwise, I don't need them." He returns the glasses to his pocket, and calls up different volunteers to undo his blindfolds. Nothing has shifted at all under the black velvet bag, and the knots are so tight the men can hardly undo them. And when they finally take the dough off Kuda Bux's eyes, he says, "You'll notice that my eyes are still closed, and the imprint of them closed has been preserved in the dough."

He closes with a question and answer period. The most prevailing question, of course, is, "*How?*"

Kuda Bux has been developing his powers of concentration for years. Anyone can do this, he says. You develop this concentration by staring at the gap between the candle flame and the candle. He tells the people that it will take about twenty years for them to see results, however.

      The people leave. The entire evening was free, and they have a new idea of the world. One of the most amazing things about this man was that all he wanted to do with his incredible powers was to tell other people about it, and encourage them never to limit themselves.

⌊ Lighthouses ⌋
don't go running all over the island
looking for ships to save;
they just stand there,
shining.

-Anonymous

On
CELLS

Henrietta Lacks may have been one of the greatest contributers to medical science in the last century. But she wasn't a doctor, or an inventor. In fact, she never even knew how she helped countless others. She was only a common woman who lived in Virginia during the middle of the 20th century.

In January of 1951, Henrietta was diagnosed with cervical cancer. She fought a determined battle with the disease for about a year, before she passed away in October.

However, her incredible story begins after this. Her doctor, curious about the disease, removed samples of her cells in and around the tumor. To his astonishment, while Henrietta's healthy cells were normal, her cancer cells were not. They were like nothing the doctor had ever seen before. Normal human cells, even cancerous types, die after a few days, and are very fragile. But these cells reproduced quickly, and never seemed to die. The cells were named HeLa cells, a combination of her first and last name.

The doctor was baffled by these cells,

which were not dying and were extremely strong. They were so hardy they could survive being sent by US Mail around the country, which the doctor did to ask his colleagues' opinions on the phenomenon. Not even the most prominent doctors today are capable of explaining Henrietta's extraordinary cells.

    HeLa cells, because of their longevity and hardiness, have been used extensively for research and experimentation. The cure for polio was developed and tested on HeLa cells, as well as many other diesases. They have reproduced so many times that it is estimated the combined weight of these microscopic cells is more than Henrietta Lacks weighed while she was alive.

    Henrietta Lacks was an incredible woman and is still mostly unknown, though the contribution she made to medical science has been immeasurable.

In the human relationship,
distance is not measured in miles,
but in affection.
Two people
can be right next to each other,
yet miles apart.

-Unknown

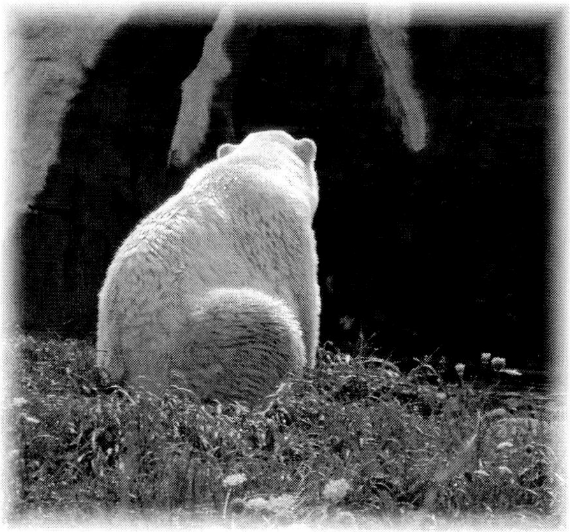

On
MARTIAL ARTS

A young man had recently been studying martial arts, and wanted to practice his new skills. He went into a big city, where he knew he would find lots of people. But his teacher had told him that he must never start a fight, and only wait for the fight to come to him. So he waited.

He was riding aimlessly on the subway when the doors opened and a drunken man came onto the train. He careened down the aisles, shoving people out of the way. He kicked a businessman's briefcase, and it slid across the aisle. "Hey!" The man with the briefcase yelled, standing up. The drunk swung at him with his fist, but the businessman easily ducked it.

This is my chance! Thought the martial art student. He stood up, straightening his coat and brushing off invisible lint as he prepared himself.

But by the time he stood and walked over, the drunken man had sat down next to a small man. As the young student watched, the once crazed man lay his head down in the lap of the total stranger as he spoke to him softly, calming him.

The student returned to his seat. *Today, he thought, I have seen a real master of the martial arts.*

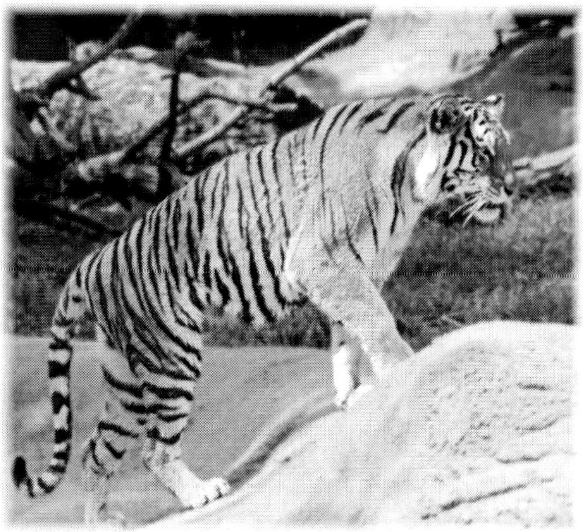

Those who call
peaceful revolution
impossible
will make
violent revolution
inevitable.

- John F. Kennedy

On
SONG

Along the coast of the Baltic sea in northern Europe, a tiny nation called Estonia was involved in an uprising that could change the way we think of revolution.

Estonia has a long history of being controlled by foreign countries. First occupied by the Swedish, the country was later taken over by Russians right before World War II. During the war, control of the country flipflopped between Nazi Germany and the USSR before it was finally declared a part of the USSR in 1944.

The USSR then began a process of "Russification." They killed many Estonian citizens, and deported nearly 20,000 people to work camps in Siberia. Then the USSR sent Russian workers to take over the government and take the jobs of the many Estonians who had been deported.

A set of harsh rules was imposed, making it harder and harder to live in peace in Estonia. Strict curfews were enforced, and any show of patriotism, including singing the native songs, was forbidden.

The people lived in fear for 45 years. But finally, in 1984, they started to strain against the harsh barriers put around them.

The Estonians were tired of being supressed, so they began to protest. They started by doing one of the smallest things the Soviets had forbidden: singing native songs. People gathered and sang what had been the Estonian national anthem, *Land of My Fathers, Land That I Love*, and because it was sung in native Estonian and not Russian, the Soviets didn't understand that singing the song was bringing about a feeling of patriotism for the Estonians. Then the protests began to grow in scale. What had started out as a few singers became thousands.

They were not allowed to fly the Estonian flag, which is three stripes of blue, white, and black, so instead they flew three flags, one of each color. Because this was not technically against the law, the Soviets chose not to do anything to stop it.

In 1985, Mikhail Gorbachev introduced two new principles hoping to help the failing Soviet economy. These were *glasnost* (openness) and *perestroika* (restructuring), and they gave the Estonians even more freedom to express their desire for independance.

The USSR had not been paying attention to the Estonian protests. But in September of 1988, they had no choice but to admit the patriotic spirit was growing. On the 12th of September, a massive song festival was held in Tallinn, the capital. Over 300,000 people, about a third of the population, gathered to sing, and their voices filled the entire city.

The Soviets were scared that they were losing control of Estonia, but confused because no war for independance had been officially declared. In 1989, they sent several tanks and military reinforcements to quiet down the unrest. But when they arrived at the Estonian border, they found something extraordinary.

Over two million people had gathered, not only from Estonia, but from its neighboring countries, Latvia and Lithuania. They all linked hands, and they began to sing as loud as they could. They stretched along the border of the country, on a major road called Baltic Way, and formed a human chain that was 370 miles long.

The commander of the tanks ordered the squadrom not to run over the people to get into the country. To this day, we don't know if he had some strategic reasoning behind this order, or if he just couldn't bring himself to bulldoze people who just wanted freedom. The tanks turned and retreated.

Within a year, Estonia had proclaimed

independance. The Soviet goverment was forced out, and a new government was set up, a free democracy. In 1991, Estonia was totally free from Soviet rule.

Not one person was killed during the entire three-year revolution. And their only weapon was song.

Necessity is not an established fact, but an interpretation.

-Friedrich Nietzsche

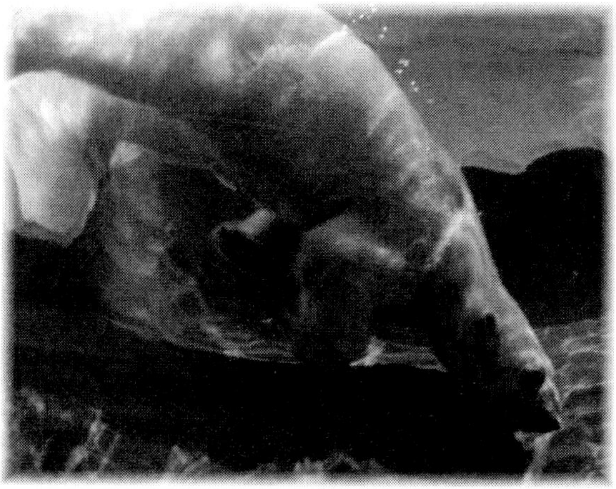

On
NECESSITIES

"I feel no need for food or water," says Prahlad Jani. Jani is a man living in India with an impossible claim: he has not had anything to eat or drink for 65 years.

When Prahlad was seven, he ran away from home in search of spiritual enlightenment. He was not discovered again until over fifty years later, living in a cave in India. During this time, he had not consumed any form of food or fluids. When he was found, he was seventy-five.

He says that when he was eleven, the goddess blessed him. "I get my nourishment from an elixir that enters my throat from the back of my palate," he says.

Every day, Jani goes into a state of meditation called Samadhi, which is characterized by complete inner bliss and extreme light and strength. He has never experienced any medical problems. He said that he did not speak to anyone for a period of forty five years.

In 2003, after much coaxing, he agreed to let a group of advanced doctors perform medical tests on him. The research group was headed by a Dr. Sudhir V. Shah, and was a team of twenty-one specialists. At first, Jani was kept in the ICU for twenty-four hours. After this, he was kept in a sealed room, with video surveillance and a guard to make sure that he did not eat, drink, or pass urine or stools. To assure that there was no intake of water, he even agreed not to bathe. To the astonishment of the doctors, at the end of the ten days, they released him in exactly the same, healthy state in which he had entered the hospital.

The average human can only stay alive for about three or four days without water. But at the end of the study on Prahlad Jani, the doctors were not able to disprove his claims. The following is an excerpt from the team's concluding medical report.

1. The protocol was strictly adhered to.
2. Mr. Jani has not passed or dribbled urine these 10 days.
3. He has not taken anything by mouth or any other route, not even water, for these 10 days.
4. All his parameters remained within the range determined by

the committee.
5. He has shown evidence of the formation of urine, which then seems to be reabsorbed into his bladder wall. However, at present, the committee does not have a scientific explanation for this phenomenon at this time.

"We are surprised as to how he has survived despite above particularly without passing urine for 10 days and remaining generally physically fit. However, it should be made very clear that we have confirmed the claim over 10 days only and we as scientists and responsible doctors cannot say anything regarding validity of the claim of his sustaining without food, drinks, urination and excretion of stools over several years."

To navigate
you must be
brave,
and to be
brave,
you must
r *e* m *e* m *b* e *r*.

-Pius Mau Piailug

On
NAVIGATION

In 1976, a group called the Polynesian Voyaging Society was doing research. They wanted to know whether ancient settlers had been able to travel from Hawaii to Tahiti, through 2500 miles of open ocean. They obtained a beautiful double hulled Polynesian canoe, which they named *Hokule'a*, or Star of Gladness, to put their question to the test. The only problem was that there was no one to captain her.

Then Mau Piailug stepped up. He was 46, and the only remaining navigator who knew the Polynesian art of sailing by the stars.

Mau was born in 1932, on the small Micronesian island of Satawal. He'd been trained in navigation from the time he was one year old. His grandfather would place the little boy in tide pools, letting him feel the pull and currents of the ocean.

Mau took the opportunity to sail the *Hokule'a* for one reason: to find interested people to whom he could pass down his knowledge. Since he was initiated as a full *palu*, or navigator, at age eighteen, no one had followed in his footsteps, leaving him the sole keeper of a huge wealth of knowledge about the ocean, sailing, and the stars. Usually, the navigators don't like to share their knowledge with outsiders. But the next generation on the islands where Mau grew up showed no interest in learning the art of navigation. They'd become too entranced with Western culture, and no one but him seemed to care that this ancient art was dying out.

On his voyage from Hawaii to Tahiti, Mau used no compass, sextant, maps or charts. He didn't operate on longitude or lattitude or mathematical equations to find his location. All he used were waves, birds, and the web of stars over his head. Every day he watched them move east to west, from their rising to setting positions. He knew over a hundred stars by name, light, color, and habit, and other stars associated with the main hundred or so. He seemed to hold the whole cosmos inside himself, with his head as the celestial hub.

Sailing in the small canoe for over a month, Mau was able to keep track of all the stars and his position relative to them. On the 31st day of the voyage, he spotted a flock of small white birds, signalling to him that his journey was almost over. He was welcomed by 17,000 people

– half the population of Tahiti.

His voyage earned him some attention, and soon he had acquired many new students. He taught them seriously, and only to a select few passed on the "Talk of the Sea" and the "Talk of the Light." In doing so, he broke an ancient law that said the sacred knowledge should be kept to the Micronesians only, but he believed the Polynesians and Micronesians were one people united by the vast ocean that surrounded them.

He made three more voyages with the *Hokule'a* in his life, and managed not only to sail across thousands of miles of open water, but to reconnect the Polynesians and Micronesians to their heritage. Revived interest in the art of navigation brought back canoe building and navigational studies to Hawaii, Tahiti, New Zealand, Raratonga, and Mau's own birthplace, Satawal.

In 2007 Mau was gifted with a double hulled canoe called the *Alingano Maisu*, whichs means "ripe breadfruit blown from a tree." The breadfruit was a favorite of his, but the word *maisu* also means " something good that is communally shared," like the knowledge of how to sail under the stars.

Mau Piailug passed away in 2010 at the age of 78, and left behind a legacy of cultural heritage and new extraodinary navigators.

All,
everything that I understand,
<u>I understand only because I love.</u>

-Leo Tolstoy

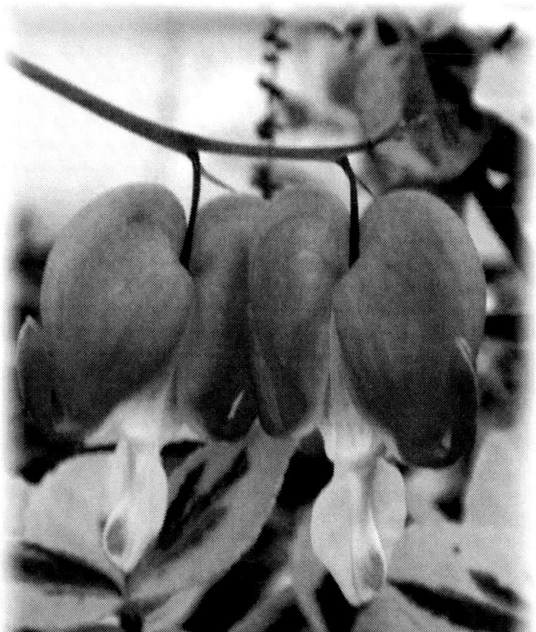

On
__HEART__

The heart is the place where your mind connects to your body. People who use their bodies in amazing ways, such as many individuals within these stories, are in a sense always acting in sync with their heart.

The human heart is much more than just the meaty blood pump it was throught to be for many years. Studies have shown that the heart itself is 60% neurons, cells that are designed to trasmit information. Recently, a discovery was made that the heart helps regulate many body's processeses through the release of different hormones and hormone-like substances.

Here's a small example of heart versus brain: point to yourself. Say something like, "I'm reading this book," and point to yourself. Now look at your finger. Where is it pointed? If you are like most people, you are pointing to your heart. You do not point to your brain, despite scientific evidence that the brain is where your consciousness is.

The heart has a magnetic field that is forty times stronger than that of the brain. When you are standing near someone, even just a normal conversational distance, your heart's field is connecting with whoever is nearby. If you are interacting with or nearby another person, sometimes the fields will exchange information and your heart rates will begin to synchronize.

This special ability of the heart to sync itself with another is learned as an infant. The baby's heart synchronizes with the mother's, especially during breastfeeding, where the baby is most entwined in the mother's magnetic field. If it does not connect this way, the baby's heartbeat may become chaotic and irregular. Children who bond successfully with their mother early in life will often have much more natural ability to connect and feel other's feelings later in life.

There was a study done on a group of meditators to show this phenomenon of synced heart rates. These meditators had been together as a group for several years. When they began to meditate, all their heart rates synced into the same steady rhythm. This was even true when the group was separated. If a member was in a different room or building, when meditating in conjunction with their group, their heart rate would sync.

"The heart is unlimited," says don

Alberto Taxo. "By opening it, you can see anything, anywhere."

Rudolf Steiner said that during the next phase of human evolution, the heart will be understood as an organ of perception.

When you allow yourself to live with heart consciousness, you will be surprised at the many coincidences that will occur. You might meet someone right when you need that person most. You might bring something with you, without knowing why, and then run into someone who needs it.

Our society has become out of touch with our hearts mostly because we are disconnected from our own feelings. Many people do not allow themselves to fully feel and express.

Our challenge is to keep our hearts open. If we are willing to open ourselves, we will experience the full power of our own hearts and beings and begin to live miraculously, going beyond all limitation to merge effortlessly with universal possibility.

FURTHER READING

- *The Biology of Transcendance: A Blueprint of the Human Spirit* – Joseph Chilton Pearce
- *The Last Navigator* – Steve Thomas
- *Zen in the Martial Arts* – Joe Hyams
- *Life and Teaching of the Masters of the Far East* – Baird T. Spaulding
- *The Singing Revolution* – Priit Vesilind with James and Maureen Tu
- *Firewalk: The Psychology of Physical Immunity* – Jonathan Sternfield
- *Encounters with Men of Miracles* – Mayah Balse

ACKNOWLEDGEMENTS

There are so many people who helped this book come into being. All your help was immeasurable, and the motivation and excitement of having others share my dream was inspiring.

To Lori Schultz, my mentor, editor, planner, scheduler, deadline maker, deadline delayer, go-to, and all around motivsator. You got the ideas of out my head and onto the page – I could not have done it without you!

To Bonnie Tout, who had no end of stories to tell, resources to lend, and inspiration to send along.

To my dad, also known as the World's Best Editor Ever and Premier Inspirational Story Finder (WBEEPISF).

To my mom, who showers me with hopefulness for what I'll accomplish each day, but is also fine with laying around and watching Pushing Daisies.

To – well, so many people! How about I end with this:

To you, the reader. I couldn't have

acheived this without you!

ABOUT THE AUTHOR

Serena Rosemary Scholz lives in Michigan with her family and a lazy cat. She is unduly obsessesed with coffee, cheese and books. She goes to school for a living, but her free time is spent writing books (such as this one), kayaking, working with horses, reading, experimenting with piano and guitar, photographing, exploring deer trails deep in the forest, and finding hidden treasures.

Interested in getting more copies of the book?
Visit www.beyondpossibility.webs.com

or

email the author at
serenacatrm@ymail.com